Jean Valentine

THE UNDER VOICE

selected poems

SALMON POETRY

Reprinted by permission of Yale University Press:

"First Love", "Miles from Home", "To Salter's Point", "Sasha and the Poet", "The Second Dream", "September 1963", "Sex" and "Dream Barker" from Dream Barker and Other Poems by Jean Valentine. Copyright 1965 by Yale University Press.

Reprinted by permission of Farrar, Straus and Giroux:

"Rebecca, 14", "Dufy Postcard", "Forgiveness Dream: Man from the Warsaw Ghetto", "Turn", "Silences: A Dream of Governments", "The Messenger", "Osip Mandelstam: 394", "Turn (2): After Years", "December 21st" from The Messenger by Jean Valentine. Copyright 1974, 1975, 1976, 1977, 1978, 1979 by Jean Valentine.

The poems from Pilgrims, Ordinary Things, Home. Deep. Blue and The River at Wolf are reprinted by permission of Jean Valentine.

Published in 1995 by
Salmon Publishing Ltd,
Upper Fairhill, Galway

© Jean Valentine 1995

The moral right of the author has been asserted.

The Publishers gratefully acknowledge the support of The Arts Council.

A catalogue record for this book is available from the British Library.

ISBN 1 897648 44 8

Cover: detail of a painting by Barrie Cooke
Cover design by Poolbeg Group Services Ltd
Set by Poolbeg Group Services Ltd in Goudy
Printed by Colour Books, Baldoyle Ind Est, Dublin 13.

Acknowledgments

My deep thanks to Mary and Bernard Loughlin at the Tyrone Guthrie Centre at Annaghmakerrig, and to the Arts Council for Artflights.

Books by Jean Valentine

Dream Barker
Pilgrims
Ordinary Things
The Messenger
Home, Deep, Blue
The River at Wolf

For Carmel, Catriona, Kerry, Mark and Pat

Contents

From
The Messenger (1979)

From
Home. Deep. Blue (1988)

From
The River at Wolf (1992)

From

Dream Barker and Other Poems (1965)

First Love

How deep we met in the sea, my love,
My double, my Siamese heart, my whiskery
Fish-belly, glue-eyed prince, my dearest black nudge,
How flat and reflective my eye reflecting you
Blue, gorgeous in the weaving grasses
I wound round for your crown, how I loved your touch
On my fair, speckled breast, or was it my own turning;
How nobly you spilled yourself across my trembling
Darlings: or was that the pull of the moon,
It was all so dark, and you were green in my eye,
Green above and green below, all dark,
And not a living soul in the parish
Saw you go, hélas!
Gone your feathery nuzzle, or was it mine,
Gone your serpentine
Smile wherein I saw my maidenhood smile,
Gone, gone all your brackish shine,
Your hidden curl, your abandoned kill,
Aping the man, liebchen! my angel, my own!
How deep we met, how dark,
How wet! before the world began.

Miles from Home

Grown, and miles from home, why do I shy
From every anonymous door-slam or dull eye?
The giant-step, the yawn
That streaked my dreams twenty years ago are gone;
The hero and nurse, the smashing Rubens hoof
And fist, the witch who rode my bedroom roof
And made my finger bleed, after all are man and wife
Whose mortal ribs I cracked to water my life,
Whose eyes I weighted keeping my late hours,
Loving my boys, chain-smoking in late, dead bars,
Watching the first light pickle Storrow Drive.
Why did I need that empty space to live?
The hand in the dark was my own, God knows
          whose cars.

The clay gods lean, and cast shadows under the stars,
Enjoying the blameless flowers on their Boston roof.
The watering-can's bland nozzle gleams like a hoof.

To Salter's Point

In Memory of Frances Valentine, 1880–1959

Here in Framingham, black, unlikely
Wheel spoking into mild Republican townships,
I have come to where the world drops off
Into an emptiness that cannot bear
Or lacks the centre to compel
The barest sparrow feather's falling.
Maybe our mortal calling
Is, after all, to fall
Regarded by some most tender care:
But here, the air
Has grown too thin: the world drops off
That could imagine Heaven, or so much care.

Framingham is building. The savage ring
And shake of the drill turn up your morphined sleep.
I fall, still in earth's monstrous pull,
To kiss your hands, your planeless face.
Oh, you are right
Not to know your death-bed's place;
To wander in your drugs from Framingham
To Salter's Point, the long rock beaches where
You and your brothers peeled oranges and swam
While your parents looked on in daguerreotype.
Your iron bedstead there was white like this:
And in this grave, unspeakable night,
Beyond the pull of gravity or care,
You have no place:
                              neither do we:

You have taken the summer house, the hedge,
The brook, the dog, our air, our ground down with you,
And all the tall gray children can run
Away from home now and walk forever and ever
And come to nothing but this mouthful of earth,
All endings over.

Sasha and the Poet

Sasha: I dreamed you and he
Sat under a Harvard tree being interviewed
By some invisible personage. You were saying
'They sound strange because they were lonely,
The seventeenth century.
That's why the poets sound strange today:
In the hope of some strange answer.'
They you sang *'hey nonny, nonny, no'* and cried,
And asked him to finish. *'Quoth the potato-bug,'*
He said, and stood up slowly.
'By Shakespeare.' And walked away.

The Second Dream

We all heard the alarm. The planes were out.
And coming, from a friendly country. You, I thought,
Would know what to do. But you said,
'There is nothing to do. Last time
The bodies were like charred trees.'

We had so many minutes. The leaves
Over the street left the light silver as dimes.
The children hung around in slow motion, loud,
Liquid as butterflies, with nothing to do.

September 1963

We've been at home four years, in a kind of peace,
A kind of kingdom: brushing our yellow hair
At the tower's small window,
Playing hop-scotch on the grass.

With twenty other Gullivers
I hover at the door,
Watch you shy through this riddle of primary colors,
The howling razzle-dazzle of your peers.

Tears, stay with me, stay with me, tears.
Dearest, go: this is what
School is, what the world is.
Have I sewed my hands to yours?

Five minutes later you and Kate and
Jeremy are dancing. Glad,
Derelict, I find a park bench, read
Birmingham. Birmingham. Birmingham.
White tears on a white ground,
White world going on, white hand in hand,
World without end.

Sex

All the years waiting, the whole, barren, young
Life long. The gummy yearning
All night long for the far white oval
Moving on the ceiling;
The hand on the head, the hand in hand;
The gummy pages of dirty books by flashlight,
Blank as those damaged classical groins;

Diffusion of leaves on the night sky,
The foreign, sublunar walks.
And the words: the lily, the flame, the truelove knot,
Forget-me-not; coming, going,
Having, taking, lying with,
Knowing, dying;
The old king's polar sword,
The wine glass shattered on the stone floor.

And the thing itself not the thing itself,
But a metaphor.

Dream Barker

We met for supper in your flat-bottomed boat.
I got there first: in a white dress: I remember
Wondering if you'd come. Then you shot over the bank,
A Virgilian Nigger Jim, and poled us off
To a little sea-food barker's cave you knew.

What'll you have? you said. Eels hung down,
Bamboozled claws hung up from the cracking weeds.
The light was all behind us. To one side
In a dish of ice was a shell shaped like a sand-dollar
But worked with Byzantine blue and gold. *What's that?*

Well, I've never seen it before, you said,
And I don't know how it tastes.
Oh well, said I, if it's bad,
I'm not too hungry, are you? We'd have the shell . . .
I know just how you feel, you said.

And asked for it; we held out our hands.
Six dollars! barked the barker, *For This Beauty!*
We fell down laughing in your flat-bottomed boat,

And then I woke up: in a white dress:
Dry as a bone on dry land, Jim,
Bone dry, old, in a dry land, Jim, my Jim.

From

Pilgrims (1969)

Fireside

The fox went under the garden
thinking. The watersnake
never moved, or the sun.
– Night, and everyone's straight out

longing; the cat's in the woods,
the children lie loose in stories
tall as this world could
be if we could run for it Lord

Fox. Foxfire will out, we thought,
you and I, blue grass at the fire-side
side by side,
word for word,
wood for wood,
desire for desire,
nicer than God.

Orpheus and Eurydice

'What we spent, we had.
What we had, we have.
What we lost, we leave.'
– Epitaph for his wife and himself,
   by the Duke of Devon, 12th century.

Orpheus: You. You running across the field.

               A hissing second, not a word,
               and there it was, our underworld:
               behind your face another, and another,
               and I

               away.

Eurydice: – And you alive: staring,
               almost smiling;

               hearing them come down, tearing
               air from air.

16

'This dark is everywhere'
we said, and called it light,
coming to ourselves.
                              Fear
has at me, dearest. Even this night
drags down. The moon's gone. Someone
shakes an old black camera-cloth
in front of our eyes.
Yours glint like a snowman's eyes.
We just look on, at each other.

What we had, we have. They circle down.
You draw them down like flies.
You laugh, we run
over a red field, turning at the end to blue air,
– you turning, turning again! The river
tossing a shoe up, a handful of hair.

Separation

i

OK my child, said the quiet priest.
But I can't take back
the smudge of black
under his eyes, their eyes,

or turn it back to the quiet, best
time we sat
in the front room; dumb,
dressed, affectionate.

ii

*There is fear there, but you know
it's fear.* Why,
summer's just going to be starting;
I have work,
I have friends,
I have whatever I had.

I mean to take hold
like a tree. There's tar,
bolts, wires. Leaves.

The trees rattle all around.
Jack and Elizabeth live in a hidden house
and hold hands in it;
they smile at me as if in the past,
as if kindly. Jack and Elizabeth will you marry? Jack is

rubbing her back
down in front of the summer fire,
her eyes are apple green.

Out of the blue, your face
bent over some book you love.

To bed. Sheet lightening on sheet glass, a morning
enough. Enough
I don't understand:

these wires. The white
wet root here
now. These people's bread.

iii

The children make spy-maps of the neighbors for you
and paste leaves on. The river wind blows the leaves,
the neighbors rock on cinders hour to hour,
hot. I watch nights from my sliding corner
out to where you are: the street, where your
back goes walking, talking,
talking. You take daylight,
and the law, what makes things tick.
And us, wherever you go, – leaves,
how we float, and stick!

iv

Breaking. I just sit. Well,
I hear noises.

I hope to hear noises, wishes
lip up over the steps all night:

flying fish,
my own breathing.

Without knowing anything,
without money, America,
without leaving,

coming to a new country.
My two hands,
a few names.

Over and over without a smile
the little walls break up and bleed
pure violence and mend and mend.

Dream Interview with Stravinsky

"Gossip is travel,
and in these times, like travel,
speeded up to the nth degree,
and that's all right,

if you remember, of an afternoon,
the immeasurable sift
of geological time, the slowness
of say, slow snow,

                    gossip deriving
from the ancient aramaic
word, *sari*, or *safari*,

meaning
to travel,
or, to love."

Visiting Day at School

*'She knows she can rub some of her
brown skin off and use it for coloring.'*
– A mother, to Robert Coles

The tall, good, raw-boned, wrong
teacher teaches wrong
glory the children shuffle back from dumb

as we do, too,
having got the problem
right:

what you hold
in your hand
is your hand:

You shall all have prizes, and the last,
they say, first: to come home free,
warm and bare, to laugh to see, Jack,

see the years run
around the tree
to melt to feed you,

Jane, see the line the days flew,
quick bird, down around the thumb,
almost straight,

through all the king's gold,
back,
to you.

Photograph of Delmore Schwartz

A young king,
oak, painted and gilded, writing

no one should be so unhappy,
holding his hands out,

but his arms are missing from the shoulders down,
his right side's gone, his mouth's

flaking like a mirror, still
photograph of your childhood,

your son. No one
should be so unhappy, should lie

still in that bending room
where all the atoms fly

off their hooks, animals and children
and friends kill, it was a delusion,

we were not living, the hotel floor
wasn't coming and going and coming

at that great head lying flat out, gray,
waiting for the slow police.

Night

From this night on God let me eat
like that blind child on the train
touching her yogurt as I'd touch a spiderweb
the first morning in the country – sky red –

holding the carton and spoon to her mouth
with all her eyeless body, and then
orientally resting, the whole time smiling
a little to one side of straight ahead.

Pilgrims

Standing there they began to grow skins
dappled as trees, alone in the flare
of their own selves: the fire
died down in the open ground

and they made a place for themselves.
It wasn't much good,
they'd fall, and freeze,

some of them said
Well, it was all they could do,

some said it was beautiful, some days,
the way the children took to the water,
and some lay smoking, smoking,

and some burned up for good,
and some waited,
lasting, staring
over each other's merciful shoulders,
listening:
            only high in a sudden January thaw
or safe a second in some unsmiling eyes
they'd known always

whispering
Why are we in this life.

From

Ordinary Things (1974)

After Elegies

Almost two years now I've been sleeping,
a hand on a table that was in a kitchen.

Five or six times you have come by
the window; as if I'd been on a bus

sleeping through the Northwest, waking up,
seeing old villages pass in your face,

sleeping. A doctor and his wife,
a doctor too, are in the kitchen
area, wide awake. We notice things
differently: a child's handprint in a clay plate,
a geranium, aluminum
balconies rail to rail, the car horns of a wedding,

blurs of children in white. LIFE shots
of other children.   Fire to paper; black

faces, judge faces, Asian faces; flat
earth   your face   fern   coal

"Autumn Day"

Who has no house now will not build him one . . .
Will waken, read, and write long letters . . .
– Rilke, Autumn Day

The house in the air is rising, not
settling between any trees.
Its lines may have come here by machine,
wirephoto, they soften to dots in the rain.

What draws you on so hard?
            You would like to think
about resting
a minute on the mobbed walk or
the electrocardiograph table
            to ask about the house there – dark,
            stone, floating out over the edge of the buildings,
            someone, something, it may be, inside –
but you can't stop here: the dangerous air,
the crowds, the lights, the hardening Indian Summer . . .

            strange quiet,
with time for work, your evenings, you will write long
            letters
this winter, you have your friends,
and the names of friends of friends.

He said,

"When I found where we had crashed, in the snow, the
        two of us,
alone, I made a plan. It takes all my energy to like it.
The trees keep thinning, and the small animals.
She swims over me every night like warmth, like my
        whole life
going past my eyes. She is the sleep they talk about, and
        some days
all I can want is sleep."

Forces

This man, blind and honored,
listens to his student reader;
this man did what he thought he should do
and sickens in jail; another
comes to the end of his work;
another threw himself out.

Us too, our destinies get on,
into middle age.

Today we visited a field of graves –
slaves' or Indians' graves, you said –
sunk, unmarked, green edges of hammered granite
sharp as a shoulder blade.
                                    God break me out
of this stiff life I've made.

After Elegies (2)

The doctor tells me, "Swim.
You are beginning, moving on; yes,
trailing his side, still
amazed at your own body apart; yes, looking back,
you don't have to smile that way, afraid
we are not here; you are beginning,
leaving nothing; your friend is here
with you, and you know him,
and all your old desire;
but in a strange tranquillity.
Yourselves. No reason any more
why not."

3 a.m. in New York

I have been standing at the edge
of this green field all night.
My hand is sticky with sugar.

The village winks; it thinks it is
the muscle of the world. The heart.
The mouth.

The horse is standing across the field, near the fence.
He doesn't come any closer,
even in the dark, or run away.

Blood memory:
fixed on vacancy:
coming back and back for a sign –

the flat of his coat,
the shut out of his eye.

Susan's Photograph

I am the razor that has been put away, also
the wrist in the photograph,
and – lately – also the photographer,
the friend, the taxi, the hospital room,
the three other women, their visitors, the flowers,
and the nurse.

At the end of that summer
I started going to paramedical school
at night. Days I still talk to my students
about all the dead
overexciteable poets; all their friends;
and the living; and show the old newsreels
where they keep leaving each other, old
people, children, soldiers; and the parades:
the general, the waving people, the black horses, the
black limousines, the mules, the tall gray puppets.

But this photograph here:
a woman in a country room, in western Massachusetts,
in peace, so sad and grained:
now I see you look up, outside the frame –
this room here, friends, a table, a book or two,
paper, I see you have all you need,
– *even in prison you would have your own childhood* –
see you go on and do what you ought to do,

it is enough, now,
anywhere, with
everyone you love there to talk to.

Outside the Frame

It is enough, now, anywhere,
with everyone you love there to talk to.

And to listen.
Slowly we can tell each other some things about our lives:
runs, rests, brief resolutions; falls, and lulls;
hard, joyful runs, in certainty; dull, sweet
durances, human silences;
                    look back in at the children,
the regular, neutral flicker of their blood; pale, solemn,
long-legged animal-gods in their sleep,
growing into their lives, in their sleep.

Forces (2): Song

Weeds breaking up through stone:
our hold on our own hollows, the quick,
curved line of a smile: bare, our own
ribs shelter us: a boy's cold, white
fingers around a match:
heart belling: hollow, quick,
through the live horn, the bone, to this
day, calm.

From

The Messenger (1979)

Rebecca, 14

Squat, slant-eyed, speaking in phrase-book phrases, the
        messenger
says he is your brother, and settles down on his heels
to wait, muffled in flat, supple skin, rope over his
        shoulder. You
wait, play, turn, forget. Years,

years. The messenger is both like the penguin
who sits on the nest of pebbles, and the one
who brings home pebbles to the nest's edge in his beak,
one at a time, and also like the one
who is lying there, warm, who is going to break out soon:

becoming yourself: the messenger is growing
strong, tough feet for land,
and strong wings for the water, and long
butter-yellow feather eyebrows, for looks. And will speak,
calmly, words you already know: "thread," "island,"

"want": now, slowly, just while you lie on your cot there,
        half-
dozing, not reading, watching the trees,
a summer, and a summer; writing long pages, tearing
        them up;

lying there under the close August window, while at your
        back
the water-lit, dotted lines of home start coloring in.

Dufy Postcard

The postcard taped on your white kitchen wall has roses,
in a white bowl, on the blue and green shadowed table;
the table is brown, yellow. Down the wallpaper's field of
pink roses, a violet shadow turns brown, moves across the
floor: now the lines go off the card, the lines of the walls,
one curved foot of the round table, the oblong shadow;
the floor ends mid-air, here:

> You sitting at your table
> looking at the postcard. Green
> day lights the windows; everyone
> still asleep. Taut lines.

> Day, with its hours, and buildings;
> people start, around you. You wait
> a minute more in the white room –
> white tent against the snowed-over path, the wind,
> its familiar voice – *one life* –

> Every day you move farther outside
> the outlines, kinder, more dangerous.
> Where will you be going.
> Who will the others be.

The Forgiveness Dream:
Man from the Warsaw Ghetto

He looked about six or seven, only much too thin.
It seemed right he would be there, but everything,
every lineation, was slow . . . He was speaking in Polish,
I couldn't answer him.
He pointed at the window, the trees, the snow,
our silver auditorium.

I said to him in English, "I've lived the whole time
here, in peace. A private life." "In shame,"
I said. He nodded. He was old now, kind,
my teacher's age; my mother's age. He nodded,
and wrote in my notebook – "Let it be good."

He frowned, and stopped,
as if he'd forgotten something,
and wrote again,
"Let it."

I walk, and stop, and walk –
touch the birch bark   shining, powdery, cold:
taste the snow, hot on my tongue –
pure cold, licked from the salt of my hand:

This quiet, these still unvisitable stars
move with choices.
Our kin are here.
Were here.

Turn

This is the new apartment   new
painted livingroom
its table, its bed, its chair.
It is floating, and the earth's bright rim
is floating through an indifferent blank, without
color, without consolation –

      The pregnant woman with a child at home
      rests, has a cup of tea, closes her eyes . . .
      I want to walk in the winter field again . . .
      Was peacefulness
      ever what we were after?
      She thinks of the child, who wants the tea, who wants
      her eyes, her mouth, her hands,
      who pulls her out to the field
      to the thick of things
      away from the thick of things.

A woman stands   at the new window.
Torso: a bronze Matisse back:
in the Museum garden. Its children playing, still,
inside its hollow part.
Its strength thickens, simplifies.
Grows quieter.

The first day's quiet. The second; the second
year. I'm taking up my life. If you were here
who I am honest with
I'd have to think a long time
to say the simplest thing:
nothing like anything I know.

Silences: A Dream of Governments

From your eyes I thought
we could almost move   almost speak
But the way your face
held there, in the yellow air,
And that hand, writing down our names –
And the way the sun
shone right through us
Done with us

               Then
the plain astonishment – the air
broken open: just ourselves
sitting, talking; like always;
the kitchen window
propped open by the same
blue-gray dictionary.
August.   Rain.   A Tuesday.

Then, absence. The open room
suspended   The long street
gone off   quiet, dark.
The ocean floor. Slow
shapes glide by

Then, day
keeps beginning again: the same
stubborn pulse against the throat,
the same
listening for a human voice –
your name, my name

The Messenger

I/The Father

In the strange house
in the strange town
going barefoot past the parents' empty room
I hear the horses   the fire   the wheel   bone wings
your voice.

I make my corners:
this table
this letter
this walk.

2

The night you died
by the time I got there to the Peter Bent Brigham Hospital
the guard said, It's no use your going up.
That was the first time you spoke to me dead –
from the high corner of the lobby.

The next night a friend said, Well these deaths
bring our own deaths, close.

3
But now, this is your voice
younger than mine; leaning over – *say goodbye* –
the fake gold Navy officer's sword
the square real gun.

4
Every night the freight train crossed the grown-over road
at the foot of the Neilsens' field, trailing its rusty
whistle. The fire, the wheel; fireflies.
The wall of stars. Real horses. I could go
anywhere. I could go to where you are.
I lie under the bank, my face on the wall of wet grass.
I can't go anywhere, No such thing my dear.

My mother has flour on her hands,
on her cheekbone. My father smiles his one smile
gray and white on the wall. She pushes
her hair back from her eyes. His eyes
settle. On us.

II/The Messenger

You are the messenger,
my half-brother, I have seen you before,
you have visited me before,
in the hallways of a school, a hospital,
in a narrow hotel room once,
once on a dirt road in August.

2
I lean on the oak grain of this desk,
the grain of your body, your hair,
your long back.   This plum
is darker than your mouth
I drink its salty sweetness   its leaf-smell
from your tongue. Sleep;
your dark head at my breasts
                              Turns
to a boy's head, you are Allan   my brother
Johnny DeSoto, nine
Philip   my brother
David

Your hand is my father's sure, square hand,
it is not too late, digging down through the sand
to show me the water

You turn, say something in your sleep

You are my sister   I hold you warm in my hand
her breast
You trace my breasts

3
My eyes were clenched, they are opening . . .
everything, nothing . . .
We aren't afraid.
The earth drips through us

Now I want to live forever
Now I could scatter my body easily
if it was any use

now that the earth
has rained through us
green   white
green green grass.

4
You say you came to tell me, if I live without you
I'll live. That's always been your story.

III/The Hill

The dogwood blossoms stand in still, horizontal planes
at the window. In mist. Small gray figures
climb away up the green hill. Carrying precision tools
       wrapped in oilcloth.
Some push their bicycles. Wait, I'm coming, no this time
       I mean it

now I could scatter my body
if it was any use

saying again
if you do not teach me I shall not learn

– First, you see, you must be still. Touch nothing.
Here, in this room. To look at nothing, to listen to
       nothing.
A long time. First, you see, you must open your
       clenched hands.
You must carry your mother and your father at your
       breasts.

I stand on all fours, my fur
is warm; warm organs, the male and the female.
The earth is light and warm around us.
We lick our cracked old worries
like blood away from our faces, our haunches, we
nudge each other, all our white fur, goodbye, goodbye . . .

saying again there is a last
even of last times

I wake up with one hand holding hard to the other hand.
My head rests on oilcloth. A quiet voice laughs, and says
       again,

– You were going to go without me?
That was always your story.

Osip Mandelstam: 394

Toward the empty earth
falling, one step faltering –
some sweetness, in this
unwilling hesitance –

she walks, keeping
just ahead of her friends,
the quick-footed woman,
the young man, one year younger.

A shy freedom draws her, her hobbled step
frees her, fires her, and it seems
the shining riddle in her walk
wants to hold her back:

the riddle, that this spring weather
is for us the first mother:
the mother of the grave.
And this will keep on beginning forever.

There are women,
the damp earth's flesh and blood:
every step they take, a cry,
a deep steel drum.

It is their calling
to accompany those who have died;
and to be there, the first
to greet the resurrected.

To ask for their tenderness
would be a trespass against them;
but to go off, away from them –
no one has the strength.

Today an angel; tomorrow
worms, and the grave;
and the day after
only lines in chalk.

The step you took
no longer there to take.

Flowers are deathless. Heaven is round.
And everything to be is only a promise.

– Voronezh. 4 May 1937

Turn (2): After Years

January. At the window
wet-dark twigs and branches of young birch
reach up, cross each other:
a road map, a map of rivers . . .

Hundreds of drops of the freezing rain
hold the day's gray light close:
silver   hundreds of stars

I think of you
looking out your city window – everyone away
– a thin, light-eyed, noticing child,
standing so quiet

– a tall man, restless, faithful, your light eyes always
looking away . . .

I think of our lives
different   the same

the years, half blown
What we had, we have.

Now I can turn
– now, without want, or harm –
turn back to the room, say your name:
say: *other*   say, *thou* . . .

December 21st

How will I think of you
"God-with-us"
a name: a word

and trees paths stars this earth
how will I think of them

and the dead I love   and all absent friends
here-with-me

and table: hand: white coffee mug:
a northern still life:

and you   with us
without a body

quietness

the infant's red-brown mouth   a star
at the star of a girl's nipple . . .

From

Home. Deep. Blue (1988)

Willi, Home

In memory

Last night, just before sleep, this: a bright
daffodil
lying in bed, with the sheet pulled up to its chin.
Willi, did I ever know you? The shine
in the lamplight!   of your intelligent glasses,
round and humorous.
Did I ever know myself? When I
start bullshitting I see your eyebrows fly . . . This book
is dedicated to Willi,
whom I do not know,

whom I know. The words in my head
this morning
(these words came from an angel):
"It's too late to say goodbye.
And there are never enough goodbyes."
I know: the daffodil
is me. Brave. Willi's an iris. Brave.
Brave. Tall. Home. Deep. Blue.

To Raphael, Angel of Happy Meeting

The pear tree buds shine like salt;
the stretch of new-ploughed earth holds up
five colors of brown to the strict sun –
like an old woman's open hand, at rest.

The young people of this house wake up,
one by one, they set out . . .

Further away, still their voices hold,
across the fog; and the pull of the ropes
– these branches rubbing in the rain –

Further away, the full sails   grains of salt
thrown into the wind . . .

The pear tree prints its buds
across my back, my hands,
bright drops of light, in the wind. Light,

Break through this husk, this
mask of 'Goodbye' . . .

Why was I crying? It was as if
some courteous hand
had touched my eyes, and I saw,

in that thin Sixties backyard
in Seattle, the abundant tree
open out its branches, white-gold wings
protective of our waiting,
of our wishes, still too light for us to hold.

Primitive Painting

Everyone is wearing work clothes, old clothes, boots; and old uniforms, painted green and brown, like trees. The new government has asked everyone to assemble in the centre of the Old City, and has given everyone small ribbons to wear, stiff flowers.

Two men in business suits are pouring wine into cups, at a long trestle table; a few of the men and women have begun to drink.

At the bottom corner of the painting is a row of bright green leaves, like a signature. A tall man, in the foreground, looks straight out into the painter's eyes; his hands are crossed over his genitals. There are no children, or animals, in this picture; no one makes a sound, or has another side.

This is a desert, and they call it peace, this is Liberation Day; the new government is drunk again, and the painter's fear is white in his paint.

Awake, This Summer

I see you a minute, a year ago, at the door
of our friend's empty room,
your eyes, the slanted-back weight of your body,

moseying around. That night, your hand
jumped in your sleep, you said
"Everyone was friends" . . .

Late summer mornings
I slept in your side, in the sun,
and to all your wishes in my sleep I wished "Yes."

A year's ocean of sleep we moved in,
without air; no one
was friends.

                Awake, this summer, first
finished with that, my chest hurts, and
the shallowest breath is life.

Mandelstam

1934–35. The time of his arrest and imprisonment in Moscow, and his exile, with his wife Nadezhda Jakolevna Khazina, to Voronezh.

My mother's house
Russia
Calm are the wolf's bronze udders,
calm the light around her
fur, out-starred with frost

I am 43
Moscow we will not live

Russia
Iron shoe
its little
incurved length and width

Russia   old
root cellar   old mouth of
blood under-the-earth
pulling us down into herself
no room to lie down

and your poor hand
over and over
draws my brain
back to your breast's small
campfire

Voronezh we won't live
not even my hand
to hold to your hand, useless.

The Drinker's Wife Writes Back

(A suburb, 1947)

You never hear me, your letter said.
But I was the one who always listened
and understood, reliable, listening
at your thought's door . . . I was steady
as the oak our bed is made of . . .

The name of a good doctor, your letter said.
I wait in his green waiting room;
my hands are big, pale, idle. Neutral, intent,
his secretary calls me 'Dear,'
like one of my own children.

He is kind. I can't last out the hour.
The window panes behind him stare me down,
the lenses over his eyes. He asks, What brings me here?
But I feel – not naked –
but absent, made of air

because how could I ever have told
anyone how it was, how the lighted house
went out in the gin brightness
you called 'the war' – and that I did this to you –
I did not do this . . .

Birthday Letter from South Carolina

for Sarah, 21

Yellow apple
star inside the apple
seed star   quiet

*

Walking up this quiet, red-earth road,
I think of you there, near the white-
edged harbor; in a yellow kerchief,
in the blowing sunlight, you walk
along the concrete of the holding world.

You hold it all to your chest, the blue day, night,
long reading, long talk, – You hold
your kind, stumbling, sure
life in your hands.
Indian cloth, the goose-neck desk light . . .

*

Basho spent the first thirty years of his life
apprenticing; four years alone in a small hut
on the outskirts of Tokyo;
the last ten years
walking. Walking here

today I saw him, Basho, at the far edge of the field;
and you alongside him; your steps,
his long black and white steps stirring up
red mica dust to drift across the new day's light, and the
          heat.

65

The Counselor Retires, and Then He Dies

Getting each other's jokes,
each other's absences; my first wise
practice at intimacy; and now the hero
shrugs on his London raincoat and walks away,
down the shiny street: it's a death, Doc.

No more of
you in your pale green office, your bright green pants,
your lounging, affectionate smile, you
cradling your dog when he had a cold,
the way you would cradle me, if I was a dog,
or a baby, the way God cradles us,
only we can't feel it . . .

Shea,
guard me and keep me,
as I keep you;
let me go, and I
let you go; a white balloon magic-markered *Shea*
floating up the white sky.

Juliana

Our lives went differently,
we lost touch . . .

The table is solid,
its long cloth shines.
Husband and wife lived in one house, forever,
and this was nothing wonderful, a simple fact.
Grown children gather, they bring
white tulips, forsythia.

All the guests make toasts. Sex taps at our sleeping ears
like water in another room . . .

The couples lean back, rich canvases. My hunger plays
in front of them, empty, – dozes off, day-dreaming
of true desire.
I try waking, try saying,

Well, we're all human,

                              – One outlying face smiles
and leans forward, gray and mild . . .

Later Juliana
I meet you, a minute, on the stairs,
and you stop, and hold my arms,
and tears run down your face . . .

Just waking up
she didn't remember what time of year it was,
and couldn't remember if she had a friend
in the world, Oh thank God, summer, and she
            remembered last night
her husband's friend, the professor,
that he said, Waiting is what we do, in this life, we wait.

Visit

This warm house, masculine; our old,
20-years-old hug;
your gray eyes, that I trust.
But our clear,
perfect sentences,
like money. No silences.

Jokes, books, our friends . . .
Why are you always
the older one? Why am I
a wooden girl, not
friends when we meet?

> The other one, tough, dumb,
> kind, the monologuer,
> the strange one, with no house
> – after our first fight
> we didn't have to have that fight anymore,
> or go away.

Solid perfect waves
break in and pull back.

It was as if you shouted after me,
"Can't you see my death, can't you see anything?"

Snow Landscape, in a Glass Globe

In memory of Elizabeth Bishop

A thumb's-length landscape: Snow, on a hill
in China. I turn the glass ball over in my hand,
and watch the snow
blow around the Chinese woman,
calm at her work,
carrying her heavy yoke
uphill, towards the distant house.
Looking out through the thick glass ball
she would see the lines of my hand,
unearthly winter trees, unmoving, behind the snow . . .

No more elders.
The Boston snow grays and softens
the streets where you were . . .
Trees older than you, alive.

The snow is over and the sky is light.
Pale, pale blue distance . . .
Is there an east? A west? A river?
There, can we live right?

I look back in through the glass. You,
in China, I can talk to you.
The snow has settled; but it's cold
there, where you are.

What are you carrying?
For the sake of what? through such hard wind
and light.
                    – And you look out to me,
and you say, "Only the same as everyone; your breath,
your words, move with mine,
under and over this glass; we who were born
and lived on the living earth."

Everything Starts with a Letter

Everything starts with a letter,
even in dreams and in the movies . . . Take
J. Juliana, on a summer afternoon,
in a white silk blouse, and a pale blue-flowered skirt,
– her shoes? blue? but high and narrow heels,
because she asks Sam to carry the plate of triscuits
into the garden, because she can't manage
the brick path in her heels.
"Oh could you? I can't manage the path in these heels."

J is the letter my name begins with,
O is the letter for the moon,
and my rage shines in my throat like the moon!
Her phoniness, O my double, your and
my phoniness . . .
Now what shall we do?
For this is how women begin to shoot,
we begin with our own feet, men empty their hearts, oh
the false self will do much worse than that,
to get away . . .

About Love

1
No   when you went to her
(oh when she told me so) then I turned to
her   her   her   her: emptiness:

black hollows falling over alone
under the white running water

2
"Light as milk in a child's cup,
I will hold you, at my lips
I will feed you," said the soft black pelican
about love, the mother, God the pelican,
the mother, stem of all our tenderness.

3
Ribbon of the
silver path of the milky
light on the water, how
you follow yourself across my mouth,
across my hair;

beads of water,
bright tall necklace of light, how you
thread yourself through me, through
my lips, their silk
stem.

Little Song in Indian Summer

I am
is my name and your name, *I am* is
the name we are finding,
I am is the
name who is finding us, is
(standing still in the high grass, in the hot sun)
the one I always wanted to find, is
the one I always wanted to find,
not mother, not child, oh you
I need
who are glad
I am I
with your green eyes even
with welcome, with letting go.

The King

You take the card of your self out
at the green crossroads, you
pull your name close around you.
But whose words are you speaking? Whose
money is this? Your warm
mouth on my mouth stuns me, your hand
on my breast is so bright, I
have to shut my eyes . . .

Still I won't take the card you offer,
though its coin is highly prized,
and its coin is wild,
– its coin is "Mine be mine,"
its coin is "And I will love you then,"
its coin was death
to the thirsty child
not heard but drowned in the deep sea . . .

High School Boyfriend

You were willing to like me, and I did something,
and blew it,
and your liking me would have saved me,
and my liking you would have saved you,

that was the circle I was walking around,
pushing a bar that moved a wheel
down in the dark, holding my breath,
naked in a long hard army coat of you,
hating my feet, hating my path . . .

Today my tongue is a fish's tongue,
kissing my friend's light breastbone, his chestnut down;
full of tears, full of light, half both,
nowhere near my old home: no one anywhere
is so wrong.

Tonight I Can Write . . .

after Pablo Neruda

Tonight I can write the lightest lines.

Write, for example, 'The evening is warm
and the white mist holds our houses close.'

The little evening wind walks in the field grass
and hums into her own chest.

Tonight I can write the lightest lines.
I love him, and I think he loves me too.

He first came to me on an evening like this one
and held me in his arms.

He kissed me again and again then,
under the motherly bending down stars.

He loves me, and I think I love him too.
How could one not love his calm eyes, as blue as the earth.

Tonight I can write the lightest lines.
To think that I did not know him, that now I am
            beginning to know him.

To feel the warm lamplight: soon it will warm his brown
            arm.
'And the verse falls to the soul like dew to the pasture . . .'

Trust Me

Who did I write last night? leaning
over this yellow pad, here, inside,
making blue chicken tracks: two
sets of blue footprints, tracking out
on a yellow ground,
child's colors.

Who am I?
who want so much to move
like a fish through water,
through life . . .
                    Fish *like* to be
underwater.

Fish move through fish! Who
are you?

And Trust Me said, There's another way to go,
we'll go by the river which is frozen under the snow;

my shining, your shining life draws close, draws closer
God fills us as a woman fills a pitcher.

From

The River at Wolf (1992)

X

I have decorated this banner to honor my brother. Our parents did not want his name used publicly.
– from an unnamed child's banner in the AIDS Memorial Quilt.

The boatpond, broken off, looks back at the sky.
I remember looking at you, X, this way,
taking in your red hair, your eyes' light, and I miss you
so. I know,
you are you, and real, standing there in the doorway,
whether dead or whether living, real. – Then Y
said, "Who will remember me three years after I die?
What is there for my eye
to read then?"
The lamb should not have given
his wool.
He was so small. At the end, X, you were so small
playing with a stone
on your bedspread at the edge of the ocean.

The Summer Was Not Long Enough

Stanley, my ex, the painter,
stepped out of his van.
His beard was gone. Loudly, carefully,
he started to paint the trees
and the ground and the telephone poles
grass green.

Funny, I was crying
after him: not Stan's upsidedown-ness,
my own. My own friends, not written back,
not called. Oh our love
turned from, and August half over.

August's more than half over;
Dove, it's time for peace.
Time to taste the round mountains, the white and green,
and the dusk rose of relationship, again,
for the first time, it's time to take off our clothes,
and the fortresses around our eyes, to touch our first fingers,
you and I, like God, across everything.

The Year of the Snake

I had to ask you questions: if I didn't, well
you'd think I'd robbed a bank. And then, blood all over, God,
I would've robbed a bank. But my old God,
my questions were too small for you. You
were so much older, you *knew* so much. You
used your words like bricks, whole leathery old
books black with words, to wall me out, words gold
as booze, to leave the room, leave me, leave us. Oh
since that time, I have learned
to let you go and live . . .

Nor my friend happy as God I sit down and comb your hair.
Your hair shines like honey like sex like the current in the river.
The river combs out our anger our tenderness.
Our silent tenderness not *my* or *mine* or *yours*.
Your unspeaking mouth shining.
Shining lifesnake drinking at my lips milky with life.

Bud

Christmas night, my father said, "Jean,
you are so disloyal." But Bud said,
"No. Ethereal. Ethereal, but my friend.
And I, I *got* my prayer answered:
I died with my life around me."

To a Young Poet

for Michael Klein

This January night at ten below I wish you
true desire, like a rose: to stand
in your chest. Veined. Bloom.

Let you be. Reflected in the train window,
inside a thousand circles of public darkness,
desire, a round red star.

And desire again, a foliating wand,
and you the Jack of wands.

The round red rose of sleep in bloom. This is
true desire, it lets you be.
It says, "No money here."

What does it taste like?
True desire. Eye-
shadow, cinnamon.

Foraging

1. The Room

Why did you keep finding me where I was?
Your seeking, your cage:
oh, your animus against breasts, shadowed eyelids . . .
yet like holding your breath, holding Love.

Love, you said,
come in. Love, let me in.
Everyone else was asleep.
Look at me, you said.

The luminous room.
Eve formalised.

A kiss: my fear and
my love,

not here yet,
but *for* here.

2. The Luminous Room

What it felt like:
first it was the kiss.
Look at me, he said.
And then it was the floor,
the boards. He went slow, he'd
pull and pull and pull at my leaf thirst.

Or running backwards he'd wind the kite-string lace
down out of me so the hot slow wind
would almost touch me . . . No . . . Then Jesus God,
the first room: sky, and trees,
but water: blue blue blue bloom bloom.
It was the feeling of terrible scarcity
and then it was the boards
and then it was the luminous room.

Alfred and the Abortion

Alfred, what did they do with your arm bones?
Burned, lying in ashes and clinkers,

or long arm bones lying inwards
Christian-folded fallen across your dropped
rib bones, out there on Long Island . . .

Your heavy right wrist bones
that engineered your work:
a rose, a rainbow of oil on the rowboat floor:

the baby we lost in sixty-nine, with you
in the hospital out of work when I did it
and I couldn't have told you then. Her name was Gift.

Twenty years later I dreamed last night of your wrist,
me eating your wrist, for the child to eat it,
your hand working, and the virtue of your wrist.

Redemption

for James Chace

Nan, the poet in Rome, New York, yesterday
wrote she saw the word "Confluence" in her sleep.

The run of black hair down your arm,
the deep-worn line across your polished shoe.

"Confluence": two rivers joining,
or, the longing to return:

because Jim, we parted
on either side of this green island,
Christ! it seems it was a hundred years ago.

But now there is no inside wall:
all down our bodies, from our heads to our feet,
there's only a line like light,
and all around us
a line like an eggshell of light.

Seeing You

1. Mother

I was born under the mudbank
and you gave me your boat.

For a long time
I made my home in your hand:

your hand was empty, it was made
of four stars, like a kite;

you were afraid, afraid, afraid, afraid.
I licked it from your finger-spaces

and wanted to die.
Out of the river sparks rose up:

I could see you, your fear and your love.
I could see you, brilliance magnified.

That was the original garden:
seeing you.

2.   *Lover*

Your hand was empty, it was made
of four stars, like a kite;

blessed I stood my fingers
in your blue finger-spaces, my eyes' light in

your eyes' light,
we drank each other in.

I dove down my mental lake fear and love:
first fear then under it love:

I could see you,
Brilliance, at the bottom. Trust you

stillness in the last red inside place.
Then past the middle of the earth it got light again.

Your tree. Its heavy green sway. The bright male city.
Oh that was the garden of abundance, seeing you.

The First Station

The first silver work of kindness,
my hand, your hand and your eye, and then the gold play
of watery car lights across the child's white quilt
we slept under and on top of, that February . . .

The rude walnut smell of the hibernation nest.
Sleeping I thought

If there was a hole through you
and a hole through me
they'd take the same
peg or needle
and thread us both
through the first station
and there we'd lean
and listen and listen . . .

Night Lake

He must have been one or two, I was five,
my brother Johnny's cock
floated like a rose of soap in the tub;
it had the faint, light rock of the boat
you carry in you when you're on land again
at the end of the day . . .

Oh all I've never gotten written down!
On paper, on my skin. Oh navy blue lake
that I want to drink
to the bottom. And you,
Barrie, what can I give you to drink?
Not the flask of ourselves, we already have that.

The solitude drink
in the kerosene lamplight at the caravan table . . .

The Badlands Said

I am the skull
under your hundred doubts. I, I
will be with you always.
Heart's-deprive.
Still numinous and alive.
Elephant's side.

Come lie down,
tooth and bone.

Ya, ya,
from a mile high
I crook you up warm,
rabbit-arm.

I am love's sorrow,
the desert's violet needle and gray star.

The River at Wolf

Coming east we left the animals
pelican beaver osprey muskrat and snake
their hair and skin and feathers
their eyes in the dark: red and green.
Your finger drawing my mouth.

Blessed are they who remember
that what they now have they once longed for.

A day a year ago last summer
God filled me with himself, like gold, inside,
deeper inside than marrow.

This close to God this close to you:
walking into the river at Wolf with
the animals. The snake's
green skin, lit from inside. Our second life.

The Ring

The ring was
three times too small for a finger,
even a piece of string could not go through it!
So I asked her,
Woman, why have you sold or given me this ring?
Nunlike she bobbed her white head-scarf chastisingly,
black eyes, black under her eyes, she said,
Something is being taken away.
You must keep seeing: everything
must be turned to love that is not love.
Mother,
going in to death,
can you do it: love
something that was there that is being taken away.

Barrie's Dream, the Wild Geese

"I dreamed about Elizabeth Bishop
and Robert Lowell – an old Penguin book
of Bishop's poetry – a thick china cup
and a thick china sugar bowl, square,
cream-colored, school stuff.

                 And Lowell was there,
he was talking and talking to us,
he was saying, "She is the best –"
Then the geese flew over,
and he stopped talking. Everyone stopped talking,
because of the geese."
                The sound of their wings!
Oars rowing, laborious, wood against wood: it was
a continuing thought, no, it was a labor,
how to accept your lover's love. Who could do it alone?
Under our radiant sleep they were bearing us all night long.

The Under Voice

I saw streaming up and out of the sidewalk the homeless
       women and men
the East side of Broadway fruit and flowers and bourbon
the homeless men like dull knives gray-lipped the
       homeless women
connected to no one streaming no one to no one
more like light than like people, blue neon,
blue the most fugitive of all the colors

Then I looked and saw our bodies
not near but not far out,
lying together, our whiteness

And the under voice said, Stars you are mine,
you have always been mine; I remember the minute on the
       birth table
when you were born, I riding with my feet up in the wide
       silver-blue stirrups,
I came and came and came, little baby and woman, where
      were you taking me?
Everyone else may leave you, I will never leave you, fugitive.

Come Ahkmatova

A homeless woman with harsh white hair
stands outside my Chinese-red door
blocking my way into my
home place:
She says *I lived here once.*
This is my place. I want my pictures.

I have them, the glass of the frames is broken,
if she comes in
she will be my bad ikon,
throw me away
as I throw her away, her
gray unmoving accusing stare. Come Ahkmatova
in the siege of Leningrad:
"Can you write about this?" "I can."

James Wright: in Memory

Looking back at me
from his death, from the feminine side, he asks me
to touch him on his throat, on his breastbone,
to touch the spots that have the life in them. His voice
is closer to me than I am to myself.
Unknowable, beginning in joy, his voice
is closer to me than I am to myself.

Wish-Mother

I've never felt
so close to you, Wish-Mother. Wings, oh
my black darling. Almost free.
Never felt so close to anyone. Felt,
Hide you in the shelter of my wings.
All the way home to New York my heart hurt.
Am I taking the old glass out of the frame? Are we?

I love glass because of water,
water because of blood,
blood because of your heart,
lapping against the birth door to my ear,
over and over, my darling, my familiar. And my good.
All the way home to New York my heart hurt.
(The second time you died this year.)

The Morning of My Mother's Death

A thumbnail-sized globe of blood:
an embryo:
I lose it, I can't find it.
A woman, a midwife or a companion,
says, do I *want* her to kill it?

Our mother wants to take herself
away from us. My kisses.
She loves another country
better than this.
Another class of people.
The class of the dead.

Listen listen listen:
(whisper this:)
her silk spirit is leaving the crown of her head.

The Night of My Mother's Death

for Richard McCann

The night of my mother's death:
what I saw:

They are winding a bandage all around her head. I say,
Leave holes for her eyes and mouth.
Then I look down, and I see,
my own wrist is only a spine of bones.

Then how will I listen any more?

I ask you Davoren Hanna, and you say:
"Ordinary communication is too slow
to succinctly indicate
my meaning."

I ask you Emily Dickinson,
water-spider rowing over danger and death: four white lines,
four white lines: nothing over nothing.

Second Mother

Black hair,
and the white hill,
and the one cedar tree, "like a soldier,"

the ripe hot stench of your motorcycle,
its squatting gleam . . .

Then, by the river,
Ha! Ha! I could have touched
your bright white circles,
your nipples' little red mouths,
redder than my mother's.

Black Hair, Black Hair! I was four, you were
sixteen, seventeen, half-girl, half-mother,
you held out safety like a sugar cube,
but how could I get to suck on it? in this world . . .

The Sea of Serenity

The Sea of Serenity:
my mother's body: ashes:
the appearance of land, and the appearance of water.

Books by the fireplace: gold brocade and silver:
but love, oh love. Outside the door.

Earth said, *Eat.*
Earth said, *Shame.*

Mother,
on my hands and knees,
face flat in the leaves,
I chomp after you like a horse.

Who died?
Who died?
Who died?

My Mother's Body, My Professor, My Bower

Who died? My mother's body,
my professor, my bower,
my giant clam.
Serene water, professor
of copious clay,
of spiralling finger-holes in the clay,
of blue breast milk,
first pulse, all thought:
there is nothing to get. You can't eat money,
dear throat, dear longing,
dear belly, dear fatness,
dear silky fastness: ecstatic lungs' breath,
you can't protect yourself,
there is nothing to get.

Butane

The huge aluminum airship
is gliding over us,
you and I with our children walking by Westport's
trees, seashore, gold trees, gold seashore.
I say, *What's that?* But no one sees it.
Then the second ship crashes just behind us,
spills butane lighter fluid over the field,
thinly spreading, fast, out over the next field;
we don't know, should we throw water over it
or not – which will be worse for the earth
(the earth itself isn't on fire yet,
only the corn in the field, and the next field).
The dwarf says, *Hold it!* walking up between my legs
into my body: *I'd better see the fire skin.*

At My Mother's Grave

Being told,
Go away.

So what is left?
This dark space on the road, that was a deer.
So many gifts:
her hazel eyes . . .

What day did she go away?

Walt Whitman,
visitor,
Emily Dickinson,
canoe of light,
Pablo Neruda,
radio flier,
fly me in.

We Go Through Our Mother's Things

When we started that day
to paint snow for earth
and sky for bread
then we knew it was time to light the last candle.
This ring is yours. This lamp.

Death Asphodel

– I feel like I've buried somebody inside of me
    Parts of her
    I don't remember yet
    Parts of myself I don't remember yet

– Yes you mean
    there is somebody blind and gummy
    lying next to you when you're asleep

– Yes that's it. Goodbye,
    down the elevator,
    something about flowers,
    about giving flowers. Me
    to my daughter?
    My daughter to me?
    My mother to me. Green flowers soon to bloom.

The First Angel

Fat slippery angels,
two by two,
carrying sheaves of straw
to the graveyard,
leaning sheaves of straw
on the gravestones,
straw on the frost stones.

God's hands trembled when he
touched my head,
we are so much in love:
the new moon holding the old moon in her arms.

The first angel said, Write down this:
It is time to leave your past life, leave your plumb-line, your trowel,
your layers of habitation, your perfect finds-tray.

At the Door

Seeing my daughter in the circle of lamplight,
I outside:

It is not *I*,
it is *Mother*.
(But it is *I*.)

It is the first tableau, the first
red wellspring of *I*.

Chimpanzee of longing,
outside the light,
wrap your long arms
around the globe of light,
hold your long haunches
wide open: be
ungodly I.

Yield Everything, Force Nothing

Years circling the same circle:
the call to be first,
and the underlying want:

and this morning, look! I've finished now,
with this terrific red thing,
with green and yellow rings on it, and stars.

The contest is over:
I turned away,
and I am beautiful: Job's last daughters,
Cinnamon, Eyeshadow, Dove.

The contest is over:
I let my hands fall,
and here is your garden:
Cinnamon. Eyeshadow. Dove.

Skate

Now a year after your death, fish-mother, skate,
you swim up off the surface of the earth:
your other-worldly face
not saying anything
face I can never meet
inside the inside face
not since the land came wet
out of the water, face
under all the pieces of light,
how could I get to you?
Never leave you. Please you!
Teacher, spine in my spine:
the spelling of the world
kneels down before the skate.

Guardian Angel in New York

You stood in the doorway in the snow:
Times Square, a late hour.
The sill was black with chicken's blood:
your black boots open: your glasses like O's:
you touched your finger to your lips, you said,
Here: Wisdom. Wisdom and power.

To Plath, to Sexton

So what use was poetry
to a white empty house?

Wolf, swan, hare
in by the fire.

And when your tree
crashed through your house,

what use then
was all your power?

It was the use of you.
It was the flower.

The Power Table

You, lying across the wide bed, vertical,
I, horizontal,

you, I, in a green field two green paths
flowered with xxxx's and xxxx's

you, I, lined inside
with pre-historic quarrels

old black cuts
in a wooden kitchen table

the table where you sit down with your older brothers
the table where things get settled once and for all

the cow's hip shaved down to the brand
her body divided into zones

Yes I am standing in the doorway
yes my softness and hardness are filled with a secret light,

but I want world-light
and this-world company.